Dedication

To my daddy, Anthony T. Pleasant, who was a perfect example to me of what a man should be. I miss you so much and love you with all of my heart!

To my mother, Bertha Pleasant; you loved me so much and laid the foundation for my financial success! I can't wait to see you again!

To my pulchritudinous wife Kimberly, and my children Christian, Zion, and Nacara.

To my Aunt Reva Benbow. I will never forget how you cared for me when my mother died. To the New Zion Christian Church Family. You are a true blessing in my life!

Humbly Yours in Christ,

Apostle Jamie T. Pleasant

Poems in the Verse of Life

Copyright © 2025 by Dr. Jamie T. Pleasant; Ph.D.

Biblion Publishing LLC

All rights reserved. No portion of this book may be reproduced, stored in a retrieval system or transmitted in any form or by any means — electronic, mechanical, photocopy, recording or other without the prior written authorization of the author — except for a brief quotation in printed reviews. Unless otherwise indicated, scripture quotations are taken from the Holy Bible, especially, the New International Version, King James Version, Legacy Standard Bible and English Standard Version.

First Edition / First Printing

Getting the most out of
"Poems in the Verse of Life"

Are you ready for a visceral poetic experience? Do you want to experience an ethereal journey in poetic peace, joy, and restoration that God has provided for you? Have you been in search of a spiritual tool to rejuvenate your soul? If you answered yes to any of these questions, this creative work is for you! "*Poems in the Verse of Life*" is just what you need to add to your literary collection of artistic works! Each reading presents a poem from the heart of the author as the Holy Spirit moved on him to provide an uplifting of your soul and spirit.

Poems in the Verse of Life
Synopsis

Congratulations on purchasing this work of poetry that I am pleased to share with you! Prepare yourself to draw inspiration from each poetic journey. This collection of divinely inspired poems is filled with various situations in life that we will all encounter. From moments of struggle and pain to the realization of peace, joy, and victory, I hope that this writing will bless you tremendously.

Table of Contents

He Is	15
The Beginning	23
And God Said	27
I Feel Like…	31
I Am	35
Trust Me	39
Look to the Hills	45
The Table is Set	49
Peace Be Still	55
God Has A Rep	59
I Can't Breathe	65
The Roots Of Royalty	77

[23] **Buy truth, and do not sell it; buy wisdom, instruction, and understanding.**

Proverbs 23:23 (ESV)

This Book Of Poetry Belongs To

_____

He Is

He is…

The anchor of the anointed

The resurrector of the redeemed

The obvious to the overcomer

He is the captain for the conqueror

Peace to the prayer

And the sword to the demon slayer.

He is…

Oh yes, He is…

Make sure you wake up so not to miss him in your slumber

He is the messenger of mercy

A friend to the friendless

A home to the homeless

Comfort to the comfortless

A mother to the motherless

A father to the fatherless.

He is…

A counselor to the convict

A healer to the hurt

A righteousness to the rejected

A relief to the neglected.

He is…

A prophet to the poor

A provider for those that need more.

He is…

A blessing to the curse

A comfort and a nurse.

He is…

A master of time

The only man to divide am and pm

Created B.C. and A.D.

Stepped in time, from no time, to make time

Just to save you and me.

He is…

The only one that died, went to hades to get the keys

Rose and came back to eat with the eleven

Walked through a wall and descended to heaven.

He is…

The one that will give you double for your trouble

Restore you with more, than you had before.

He is…

He will put you on public display

And at the last minute come in and save the day.

He is…

A tempest for the terrible

A relief for the righteous

Therapy for the thief

And a breath of life.

He is…

A deliverer for the derelict

A remover of your pain.

He is…

The king of confidence

The prince of perfection

The Lord of love

The piper of peace

And everlasting help from above.

He is…

My everything

My only thing

My only hope,

My only friend.

He is…

A miracle worker

He can take a little and make it a lot

And take a lot and make it a little

I'm talking about problems and being stuck in the middle.

He is…

He can take some fish and bread

AND feed 5000 heads

And turn right around

And raise somebody from the dead.

He is…

Able to take all of your sins

Erase them and watch you commit them all over again

And still forgive you.

He is…

The holder of a love that's unlimited

HIS forgiveness is forever

A king that will keep you

A brother that will stick with you.

He is…

My confidence when I'm in doubt

My happiness when I pout

And my glory when I shout.

He is…

I gotta go, but can I tell you some more?...

He can walk on water

Give sight to the blind

Preach a life changing sermon

And not leave anyone willing to believe not one step behind.

I gotta go, but can I tell you some more?...

He is the knowledge to the needy

The way of the wise

The usher of understanding

And the developer to the despised.

He is…

The indescribable divinity, within the trinity

And a satisfier for the insatiable.

He is…

Can I tell you a little bit more?...

He will find you in your pain

Restore your mind and keep you sane.

He is the King that will calm your stormy sea

With one phrase He will redirect your peril

Send a word of peace through a willing and anointed herald.

He can change who you are, where you are,

and bring you to who you were destined to be.

He is…

My Lord, My God

My Help, My Strength

My Healer

My Helper

My Deliverer

My God

He is!

Illumination

The Beginning

In the beginning was you

and after you,

there will be no other

Uniquely made

Divinely inspired

Creatively woven

Voraciously desired.

Admired by many

Complemented by few.

It doesn't matter; 'cause you will get your due.

Take your place

Take your time

It won't be long

'cause you're divine.

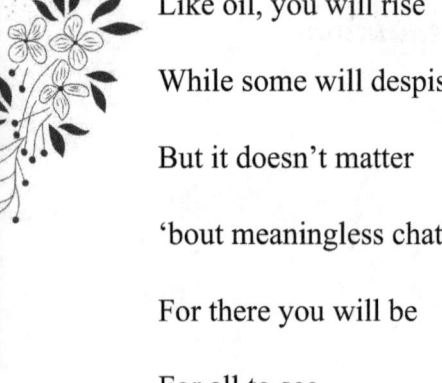

Like oil, you will rise

While some will despise

But it doesn't matter

'bout meaningless chatter

For there you will be

For all to see

That from the start

The top was your chart

And there you will stay

Each and every day

While others will say

How did you get that way?

Just reply;

There is no rhythm

There is no rhyme

I was destined for greatness

before the beginning of time.

Illumination

And God Said

In Genesis chapter one,

Creation becomes a reality based on three words,

And God said…

It all started with a word.

In these times, what we need now more than ever before is a word from God.

It will set you free and cause you to become everything you were destined to be.

To be strong

To be bold

To be thoughtful

To be forgiving, be thankful and get on with your good living.

Think about where you are

What you are going through

He's what you really need because he loves you.

So, the next time that you are down,

And your face shows a discerning frown,

Open up your ear

Hold back that tear

Open up the word and turn the leaf

Read his word and remove your grief

He's always been there

He's never departed,

You only missed Him when you became brokenhearted

Open your ear, right now, so you can hear,

He has a part

That's tailor made for your heart

Remember, and God said…

I am with you through the storm

What's happening now won't last too long

And God said, you will be blessed

And God said, it will get better

And God said, get ready for more cheddar.

And God said, let there be light

To show you the way

To not worry about tomorrow

but maximize every single day.

And God said,

you will have more money

You shall not want

Because I am God, I am with you from now through eternity

And God said,

And God said,

And it was all good.

Illumination

I Feel Like...

Some days things just don't feel right

I wake up and everything is dark that's in my sight

I try to shake it, get it off and get back up

But the more I shrug and the more I tug, the deeper I sink yet.

Yet I keep reaching, keep striving, keep looking above

Searching intently and gazing, trying to find that peace called a dove

It holds the spirit of peace, wholeness and love

The kind that can only come from heaven above

I won't give up or throw in the towel

I can feel my strength coming, I can feel my revival

I can feel my confidence, I can see my survival

I will not quit,

I will not stop,

I will not fail,

For in His arms I find my sail.

I sail on to a new place

I sail on to embrace

Embracing my dreams, embracing my life

Forgetting my pain, forgetting my strife

I feel the reward of winning this race.

I feel like goin' on!

Illumination

I Am

In times like these
You need to know
What I will do
To help you grow.

I am,
The relief in the middle of your grief

I am,
The blessing when you are stressing

I am,
The One that can change your mind
I can heal you and put your troubles behind

I am,
The one that will pay your bills

But you must ruminate and practice being still.

Then you will know me
For more than what you can get
You'll learn that with me, you will get what
you need and you won't have to sweat.

I will
keep you,
help you,

protect you and,
resurrect you.

I will give you strength
I will give you vigor
I will bless you highly
That only praise can trigger.

Praise me for what I have done

Praise me for what I will do
Praise me because my eye is always on you.

If I can provide for a sparrow

I can surely take care of you

Just a little thanks is all you need to do.
I will move your mountain
I will calm your sea

The key is to never forget
that nearer your God is the perfect place to be.

I am
I can
I will
Come to where I am.

Illumination

Trust Me

When things are rough
When the going gets tough
When there is a cloud in your present
Where you can't see
I want you to call my name and,
Trust in me.

Trust that I got you
Trust that I love you
And trust that I care
'cause all your burdens I surely can bear.

I can lift what you can't
Carry what you can't bury
Erase what you hate
'cause I'm never too late.

I won't forget
So, don't you fret

It's on its way
A much better day.

Prepare your mind
Make ready your soul

I'm going to bless you
Sit back, and watch it unfold

Ignore the news
Turn off social media

The blessing I have for you
Can't be contained in an encyclopedia.

Don't listen to the news
Don't entertain the chatter

Wait on me to hear
The conclusion of the matter.

And when it's all done
And this present administration is through
You'll look back and remember,

How good I was, taking care of you.
I've done it before
I'll do it again
I do not change,
Trust me, you are going to win!

Get ready to praise!
Get ready to shout!
Put on that big smile
Get rid of that pout
And get ready to dance and move all about!

Trust me!
Praise me!
Worship me!
Adore me!
But whatever you do,
Never forget me.

Illumination

Look To The Hills

When you are down
And no friends are around

When you are low
With no place to go

When you are tired
Facing maybe even being fired

When you have been scorned
Instead of adorned

When you have been canceled
And consistently hassled

Know that your help is just and eyesight away

Lift up your head
It's no time to act dead

Call on my name
And I will change your view

You will see things,
All the goodness that I will bring

Lift up your head
Praise me instead

Get ready to shout
Prepare for the thrill

Open up your eyes
It's there on the hill

Not only are there cattle

Not only is there wealth

Get ready for your blessing
Get ready for new health

Look to the hill

Look for my peace
Look for my joy
Look for your promised relief!

Your help is there!
Your joy is there!
Your peace is there!
'cause I am there!

Illumination

The Table Is Set

I want all to know
I want all to see
The way a divine relationship
Is supposed to be.

They will make fun of you
When you call out my name

They may even become more chatty
Especially when you refer to me as your daddy.

And when you pray
Don't be like the others
Say my son's name
Have no shame in your game.

When you do these things
In the public you'll see,
I will show them the love that exists

Between you and me.

The same ones that laughed
The same ones that joked
Will bow their heads
When your money becomes stoked.
When they see your stead
How you stand for me
In this mist of your dread

I will expand your influence
I will increase your fame

Because you lifted up my name
And you showed no shame.

So sit at the table

Enjoy your meal
It's full of joy
That no one can steal.

Sit at the table

And enjoy your peace
While others are in turmoil
You'll be relaxing from grief.

Sit at the table
And enjoy your rest
For, I am giving you from all I have
My greatest, and my very best!

You didn't deny me
When you were in public

Now, I have made every form of evil
To become your inferior subject.

Evil no longer in your life shall reign
Gone are the days of anguish and pain.

Sit at the table
Put your foot on its head
Twist it and strangle it
Until it is dead.

Illumination

Peace Be Still

In the midst of my storm,
In the midst of the rubble
I know that you will bring an end
To all of my trouble

When things are tight
And nothing seems right
I know that you will provide
because peace is within my sight

I must not flinch
I must not be scared
I must remain calm because
Your peace is near.

I can smell its aroma
I can hear its soothing voice

It is telling me to be still
and get ready to rejoice.

I won't let it pass by
I won't let it go away
I will reach out with my heart
And grab peace this precious day.

Come to me peace
Come to me joy
Come in my being
Come great envoy.
I welcome you all.

I receive you with expectancy
It's time for a celebratory ball.

Illumination

God Has A Rep

God has a rep that says He will never leave you nor forsake you!

He will supply all of your needs.

He is faithful to us even when we are not faithful to Him.

He won't give up on us even when we give up on Him.

He will keep us even when we can't find room for Him.

He says,

you won't make me look bad.

I will make you want to when you don't want to.

I will make you say yes when you want to say no,

and make you say no when you want to say yes.

Yes to my will, yes to my way.

No to that sin that you wanted to do,

It's over and done with

It's completely through.

Yes to that tithe you never wanted to give

and now you see that it's the only way to live.

You know now that your giving determines your level of living!

It's so true, you can't be God's giving.

I won't let you fail because I fail you not.

I fail not to feed you.

I fail not to clothe you.

I fail not to finance you.

I will fail not to protect you.

I fail not to heal you.

I fail not to deliver you.

I fail not because I can't fail.

Why?

For my name's sake. My name is above all names.

Above cancer,

above sickness,

above lies,

above hate,

above racism,

above wrongs!

My name is my rep.

So come on and get in step.

Go tell somebody about me.

Tell 'em how good I have been to you.

Tell 'em how I blessed you.

Tell 'em how I kept you.

Go, Tell somebody!

My word is my rep

My rep is my word,

And my word never fails!

Illumination

I Can't Breathe

I can't breathe when I work hard and walk in a bank and can't get a loan

And if I get a loan, I pay more for the loan and later wish that I had left it alone

I can't breathe when I work hard and try to buy a home,

and you charge me a complicated double-digit interest rate on a simple interest loan

I can't breathe when I work hard and try to buy a car,
and you charge me three percent more

more than you charge a white customer and

we both have the same exact good credit score

Why, oh why do you charge me more?

I can't breathe when I work hard on the same job that my white counterpart works but makes twenty percent less and he gets all the wonderful perks.

I can't breathe when I get sick with the same illness as a white person, yet he gets treated and gets better,

and all I get later is how much I owe in a quickly mailed letter.

I can't breathe when I see a new house I want to live in,

and you deny me the right to buy it based on the color of my skin

I can't breathe when I want a great education for my kids

but you refuse to provide a quality education in the zip code that I live in

I can't breathe when you intentionally rezone certain areas of the city exclusively for those that don't have anything.

You don't get that one right?

Ok, let me break it down.

In order to change a person, a person has to see and experience change.

Instead of grouping hopeless people together, put some people with hope in the middle of the hopelessness!

Then they will see what it's like to live as one that is blessed.

I can't breathe when gas costs more in the 'hood than it does in the 'burbs

I can't breathe when I am in my car and get pulled over by the police

and don't know if he is going to PROTECT me,
NEGLECT me
or DISRESPECT me!

Neglect my rights as a citizen

Disrespect my manhood

Neglect proper procedure

Neglect my life

I can't breathe when I can't get in a certain college or university because of the color of my skin.

Or, if I get in college it is because I make millions for your universities as I run and compete.

While you sit back, enjoy and relax in your seat.

I can't breathe when I realize that African Americans make up thirteen percent of the population in this nation, yet, at most universities we only comprise six to eight percent of the PWI student population.

Can't you reserve at least thirteen percent of your seats for us in your colleges?

Oh yeah, I know, it's hard to find qualified African American scholars for your colleges

However, if they are an athlete, you have no problem finding them

Somehow, some way we are right there in your sight.

If we can play sports for you, you will swim with alligators in the swamp land of Florida to find that football player.

You will comb the fields in Texas to get that Black quarterback.

You will climb the highest skyscraper in New York and Chicago, to get the next great basketball player.

It's amazing how you can find us when you have use for us to make you a dollar.

But when we want to develop as a people by becoming an exceptional scholar,
You withhold all funding and watch us just holla.

How can white Americans respect and appreciate diversity

if they aren't educated and experience it at your PWI university.

Or maybe that is the education that's taking place in American colleges, white privilege, supremacy and all that entitlement.

Hard to teach those classes with Black folk in them isn't it?

I can't breathe when I go to the store and get killed on the way trying to get back home.

I can't breathe when the person that shot me on my way back from the store
gets off Scott-free because he stood his ground as I lost mine.

I thought we all walked on the same ground. Obviously, we don't.

White ground is more precious than Black ground.
And I suffer because of my background.

I can't breathe when I go out for a jog and you hit me first with your truck

Then gun me down and you shout racial slurs as I take my last breath.

I can't breathe when the three men that murdered me, go months before they are even arrested.

As they strut through their southern town confidently innocent chested

I can't breathe when I look at my son and wonder when he leaves out the door, will he come back home or if I won't see him anymore.

I can't breathe with your throat on my neck
Can't you see that you have me in check?

Instead of removing your foot
You apply more pressure

And before you know it, I am being carried off stiff on a stretcher.

I can't breathe,

I can't

I…

Illumination

Bonus Poem

This final poem was written in 2008 at Clark Atlanta University business schools' annual *Royal Ball Gala*. I was asked to provide a poem for the occasion and I shared what I felt captured the essence of what this great business school was all about.

The Roots of Royalty

Twas' the night of the royal ball
When glitter and smiles were on them all

They came from far and near
To cherish the moments with endless cheer

To be royal is quite a title
One must be resourceful and correct in one's recital

One will find oneself always being optimistic

When overcoming challenges that can be viewed as pessimistic

See, we have something that others wish they knew

That is, what it takes to be successful that can only come from being educated in the Bschool at CAU

We think of Dr. Paul Brown when we think of being optimistic

He will waste no time teaching you about a certain supply chain logistic

Then there is Dr. Ed Davis who will show how to think and be confident in statistics

But you had better study hard and make sure you master the practical heuristics.

That humility is more than your ability, but more importantly and subserviently
Your subsistence is to place others higher than yourself on a shelf

Shelf, what shelf,
The shelf of being accountable

Accountable to the success of others,
God and this school,

Being a role model, a person of high standards, one that gives back

Slow to anger or hate, not one known to easily attack

Yes, at CAU we are royalty because we've been trained to be accountable

There is no problem that can come that we view as insurmountable

We will tackle it if comes at us

Bite it if it roars at us

Bear down on it,
if it tries to run before we are done

We won't stop unless we have won

In conclusion, by now you should know,

Here at the CAU Bschool we are legendary,

not secondary
On the contrary,
despite hard times,
good times,
bad times,
easy times
up economy
down economy,
Recession, depression,
hated, jaded,
back stabbed, front faked,

Being understood, or misunderstood,
laid off, not paid off,
hired, fired,
promoted, demoted,

Stressed, blessed,
overlooked, underpaid,
gas going up, house values going down,
losing our minds, finding ourselves,

Through all of this,
we will find a way or make one
to become legendary because we are not secondary,

on the contrary, we will always be known as a "dignitary."

WE ARE ROYAL AND COME FROM ROYALTY.
Look at the roots and path of our royalty in America.

Starting in the 1800s we were placed in a slave house;
From the slave house in the 1800s, we made it
To the outhouse
From the outhouse,
To the poor house

From the poor house,
To the shotgun house

From the shotgun house

To the shack house
From the shack house

Sadly, to the crack house
From the crack house
To the rowhouse

From the rowhouse
To the jail house

From the jailhouse
To the schoolhouse

From the schoolhouse
To a nice house

From a nice house
To the senate house

From the senate house
To the governor's house

From the governor's house, on Nov. 4th, 2008, we made it to the WHITE HOUSE!

Royalty means that you should never let your beginnings dictate your destiny.

Never let your starting point be your ending point.

I often think of greatness and legends at the CAU Bschool.

I think of the Late great Dr. Alex Williams,

Dr. Johnnie Clark,

Dr. Harding Young,

Dr. Ed Davis,

Dr. Ed. Irons,

Dr. Kasim Ali,

Professor Raphael Boyd,

Dr. Paul Brown,

Dr. Lynn Patten

Dean Silvanus Udoka

and all the professors and administrators that have served and are currently serving the students at CAU.

Wherever you are,
Whatever you are doing,
Stand up and take a pause for a ROYAL cause and salute our royal LEADERS!

Illumination

Epilogue

One of the best ways to realize the purposeful apex of reading, *"Poems in the Verse of life"* is for you to give your life to Christ Jesus. Repeat these simple words, and it will become a reality. Repeat the following: Lord Christ Jesus, as of this very moment, I accept you as Lord and Savior of my life. I now give my life to you so it can be fashioned for your purpose and glory. God, I believe everything I've said and confessed to you. I know now that I have received everlasting life based on the work that Christ has done and will continue to do in my life. Jesus, thank you for bringing me to this point where I surrender everything to you. It is in the Holy Spirit through Christ Jesus; I say Amen.

Humbly Yours in Christ

Apostle Jamie T. Pleasant

Book Dr. Pleasant

Book Dr. Jamie Pleasant for a Speaking Engagement!

For speaking engagements, please contact Dr. Jamie T. Pleasant at admin@newzionchristianchurch.org or 678.845.7055

Book Dr. Pleasant

About the Author

Apostle Jamie T. Pleasant, Ph.D., a modern-day polymath, is the founder and Chief Executive Pastor of New Zion Christian Church in Suwanee, Georgia. Additionally, he is the former dean of graduate education and currently serves as a tenured Full Professor of Marketing at Clark Atlanta University's School of Business. Notably, he is the first faculty member in the university's history to be accepted into Mensa International, the world's largest and oldest high IQ society for individuals who have scored in the 98th percentile or above on an intelligence test.

Dr. Pleasant is the first African American to graduate from the Georgia Institute of Technology (Georgia Tech) with a Ph.D. in Business Management with a concentration in Marketing, earning that degree in August 1999.

About the Author

He is a 2016 recipient of the "Lifetime Achievement Award" from former President Barack Obama of the USA for volunteer and community service. He was awarded the "Game Changer" Educator Award by Reverend Jesse Jackson at the 2019 Rainbow PUSH International Convention. As a polyhistor, in addition to obtaining a doctorate degree in Business Management from the Georgia Institute of Technology, he holds a bachelor's degree in physics from Benedict College in Columbia, South Carolina, Marketing Studies from Clemson University and an M.B.A. in Marketing from the very prestigious, Clark Atlanta University. Under his leadership, New Zion has grown from three members when it started in 1995 to well over 700 in weekly attendance, with a focus on economic and entrepreneurial development. God gave him the vision to establish a Biblically based economic development initiative for New Zion Christian Church. He remains at the pulse of the

About the Author

economic business sector in American society.

As a result, Apostle Pleasant is in constant demand to train, speak and teach others at all levels in ministry and the private sector about business and economic development across the country. He has created numerous cutting edge and industry leading ministerial, business and economic development classes and programs, along with SAT & PSAT prep courses for children ages 9-19. He founded The Financial Literacy Academy for Youth (FLAFY), where youth between the ages of 13-19 attend 12-week intense classes on financial money management principles. At the end of those 12 weeks, they receive a "Personal Finance" certificate of achievement. In 2015, he established The Young Leadership and Success Academy that teaches young people between the ages of 10-21 how to invest, make presentations and start and operate businesses. Other ministries he has pioneered include The Wealth Builders Investment Club (WBIC),

which educates and allows members to actively invest in the stock market, along with the much-celebrated Institute of Entrepreneurship (IOE), where participants earn a certificate in entrepreneurship after three months of comprehensive training in all aspects of starting and owning a successful competitive business. The main goal and purpose of IOE is that each year one of the trained businesses will be awarded up to $10,000 startup money to ensure financial success.

Apostle Pleasant has met with political officials such as former President Bill Clinton and Nelson Mandela. He has performed marriage ceremonies and counseled numerous celebrated personalities such as Usher Raymond, Terri Vaughn, and many others. Several gospel music artists have performed at the church, including Tiff Joy. Each year, Apostle Pleasant conducts chapel services for Clemson University's football team and is a

About the Author

spiritual and personal friend to its two-time national championship head coach, Dabo Swinney.

As a modern-day civil rights leader, he is a close aide to Reverend Jesse Jackson and serves on the Board of Directors of Rainbow PUSH Inc. (Atlanta) and Director of Business Education and Corporate Engagement. He serves on the Board of Fellowship of Christian Athletes (Atlanta Urban) and after the Columbine High School shooting, he founded the National School Safety Advocacy Association. His latest foundations include the Young Entrepreneurship Program (YEP) and the African American Consumer Economic Rights (AACER).

He has authored numerous books that include: *Healing from the Loss of a Loved One, Trusting God In Troubling Times, Prayer Changes Things, Powerful Prayers That Open Heaven, Capturing and Keeping the Pastor's*

About the Author

Heart, Unshakable Faith, Proverbs for Prosperity, How to release Your Blessings Through Service in Ministry, When Purpose is at Work, Today's Apostles (2024 ed.), Advertising Principles: How to Effectively Reach African Americans in the 21st Century, Discover a New You: A 21 Day Journey to Uncovering Your Uniqueness, Daily Quotes for Daily Blessings, The Making of a Man, I'm Just Sayin', From My Heart To Yours: Love Letters From A Loving Father, Today's Apostle: Servants of God Leading His People towards Unity, A 7 Day Prayer Plan for Prosperity, You Have What It Takes, A Marketing Model for Ethnic Consumer Behavior, An Overview of Strategic Healthcare Marketing and The Importance of Subcultural Marketing.

Apostle Pleasant is a lifetime member of Alpha Phi Alpha Fraternity Inc. He is the loving husband of the pulchritudinous

About the Author

Kimberly Pleasant and the proud father of three children: Christian, Zion and Nacara.

About the Author

FINI

www.ingramcontent.com/pod-product-compliance
Lightning Source LLC
Chambersburg PA
CBHW031636160426
43196CB00006B/447